UNLOCKING THE BIBLE STORY
STUDY GUIDE
VOLUME 1

UNLOCKING THE BIBLE STORY STUDY GUIDE

VOLUME 1

Colin S. Smith

MOODY PUBLISHERS
CHICAGO

Scripture taken from the *Holy Bible, New International
Version*®. NIV®. Copyright © 1973, 1978, 1984 by
International Bible Society. Used by permission of
Zondervan Publishing House. All rights reserved.

ISBN: 0-8024-6551-X

1 3 5 7 9 10 8 6 4 2

Printed in the United States of America

CONTENTS

INTRODUCTION

Welcome to the first in a series of four study guides designed to help small groups grasp the big picture of the Bible. The studies are based on the four-volume book series *Unlocking the Bible Story*. They will take you on a fascinating journey through the Scriptures.

The whole Bible is one story. It begins with two people in a beautiful garden and ends with a vast crowd in a magnificent city. Once you have grasped the main story line, you will be able to see how the individual stories of the Bible fit together, how the whole Bible points to Jesus Christ, and how God speaks through the Bible into your life today.

As you prepare for each study, you will find it helpful to read the relevant chapter from the Bible along with the chapter from *Unlocking the Bible Story* (volume 1). Then, as you gather with others to discuss what you have read, the study guide will help you to apply what you have learned. (This study guide also can be helpful for individual study and application of each chapter.)

This first study guide will take you through the Old Testament story from Genesis to Nehemiah. The study guide to volume two will take you through the rest of the Old Testament. These two studies can be completed by a small group, meeting weekly, in less than a year. When you have completed that journey, you will want to use the study guides to *Unlocking the Bible Story* volumes three and four, which will take you through the New Testament, giving you a good grasp of the whole Bible.

So welcome aboard. You are about to embark on a wonderful adventure as we unlock the Bible together. You will make many new discoveries and be led to worship as you take in the breathtaking sweep of the Bible story.

1
Life
Read GENESIS 1:1–2:25

LAUNCHING

1. What do you think most people believe to be the purpose of life? What factors lead you to this conclusion?

_____

_____

EXPLORING
The Author Takes the Stage

2. There are two options to explain our existence: We were created by God or are an accident of history. What are the implications of each?

_____

_____

3. Many in our world today believe that humans are a product of evolutionary forces. How is this affecting our view of human life?

_____

_____

Who is God

and why does

it matter?

Who am I and

why am I here?

4. If God owns you, what difference should it make in the way you live your life? What difference should it make in the way you face troubling situations?

_____

_____

_____

_____

Understanding Ourselves

5. Read Genesis 1:27. How do human beings reflect God's nature and image?

_____

_____

_____

The Kiss of Life

6. *We are made in God's image. We are totally dependent on Him for our next breath.* How do these two statements provide a healthy view of ourselves and others? Which do you need to grasp better?

_____

_____

_____

_____

Taking a Walk with God

7. Adam and Eve walked with God in the Garden of Eden. What are some of the similarities and differences between Adam and Eve's relationship with God and ours today?

_____

_____

_____

_____

A Place Called Home

8. God provided a place, a purpose, and a partner for Adam and Eve (pages 25–27). What difference does it make to know that these are gifts from God?

a. Your place _____

_____

b. Your work (including school, caring for children, etc.) _____

_____

c. Your marriage or your future mate _____

_____

Spotlight on Christ

9. Jesus said that He came to give us life to the full (John 10:10). In what ways has a relationship with Christ enriched your life?

_____

_____

_____

APPLYING

10. What is something new you learned about God or yourself from this study? How will it affect the way you live this week?

_____

_____

_____

This week, when you encounter someone who annoys you, remind yourself that the person is created in God's image. Note how it changes your view of that person.

_____

_____

_____

When praying this week, thank God for your place, your purpose, and your partner.

2
Curse

Read GENESIS 3

LAUNCHING

1. How would our world be different if sin had not entered the picture?

_____

_____

EXPLORING

Reading Your Opponent's Plays

2. Satan used three strategies to tempt Adam and Eve. Describe each in one sentence.

a. _____

b. _____

c. _____

3. How do you see these same strategies in operation today?

_____

_____

_____

If God made everything good, why is the world as it is today?

4. Which of Satan's strategies do you feel most vulnerable to? Why?

5. The sixth paragraph on page 34 describes effective defenses for each of Satan's "plays." What have you found helpful in implementing these defenses in your life?

The Knowledge of Evil/Excluded from Paradise

6. We have the knowledge of evil, and we have been excluded from the presence of God. What difference has this made to our lives and our world?

Hope That Began with a Curse/A Curse Deflected

7. Why did God find it necessary to pronounce a curse? Why did God's curse not fall directly on Adam? What evidence can you see of the curse on the ground today?

Spotlight on Christ

8. Read Galatians 3:13. How does Jesus' death on the cross relate to . . .

a. what happened in the Garden of Eden? _____

_____

_____

b. our lives today? _____

_____

_____

APPLYING

9. What is something you can do this week to shore up your defenses against Satan's schemes?

_____

_____

_____

_____

10. Do you need to adjust your expectations for life in this world based on what you learned in this lesson? How?

_____

_____

_____

_____

_____

_____

We won't truly value a prescription drug unless we realize the severity of our sickness. In your prayer time this week, recognize before the Lord the dire diagnosis of humanity. Readily admit that this was (or possibly, still is) your diagnosis. Read through the prayer on page 40 and make it your own.

3

Salvation

Read GENESIS 6:5–22

LAUNCHING

1. What thoughts and emotions would you imagine Noah felt as he completed the massive ark? When have you experienced some of these same emotions in your spiritual journey?

_____

_____

_____

_____

_____

_____

What do I

need to be

saved from,

and how can

I be saved?

EXPLORING
Building a Biblical Worldview

2. Those who hold a biblical worldview believe that

- God created them,

- that He has absolute rights over them,

- and that every good gift in their lives comes from His hand.

Describe the attitudes and actions you would expect each of these convictions to produce in those who hold them. How are they impacting you?

_____

_____

_____

_____

Amazing Grace

3. How did God express His grace to Noah? How is He doing that same thing for humanity today? Have you heeded His message? How?

_____

_____

_____

_____

_____

Deliverance Through Faith

4. How were Noah and his family saved? Why do you think the others did not get into the ark?

_____

_____

_____

_____

5. How did Noah demonstrate faith?

_____

_____

_____

_____

6. Noah faithfully communicated the message of God's judgment and deliverance. According to 2 Corinthians 5:20, what role do Christians have in making sure this message is communicated to everyone? What keeps you from communicating the message?

Spotlight on Christ

7. How is Jesus like the ark? Why do you think so many people are failing to come in?

APPLYING

8. Have you recognized that judgment is coming and accepted God's deliverance through Jesus Christ? If not, pray the prayer on page 51 and get "in Christ" today.

---

9. Ask God to bring to mind the name of someone He would like you to share the news of judgment and deliverance with.

---

10. Is there an area of life in which you need to exercise more faith like Noah? What would walking by faith look like in this situation?

4
Judgment

Read GENESIS 11:1–12:3

LAUNCHING

1. Have you ever been surrounded by people speaking a foreign language? How did it make you feel?

Why did God

cause the peoples

of the world to

speak in different

languages?

EXPLORING

Parents in Pain

2. People began to pray as they saw the sin growing in the world. Think of a time when pain led you to prayer. Describe that experience.

God Applies the Brakes

3. In John 8:34, Jesus said, "Everyone who sins is a slave to sin." How does our sin make us slaves? Can you think of some examples?

_____

_____

_____

_____

_____

4. Judgment is God's way of cutting sin back. How have you seen this happen in the course of history or in our world today?

_____

_____

_____

_____

_____

Prevention Is Better Than a Cure

5. Describe the preventive approach to sin.

_____

_____

_____

What would this mean for someone struggling with:

- greed? _____

- anger? _____

- sexual purity? _____

- other: _____

_____

The "New" Technology

6. What was the root sin of building the Tower of Babel? How have you observed this same sin today in individuals and cultures?

_____

_____

_____

7. How did the judgment at the Tower of Babel serve to cut back sin?

_____

_____

8. God's judgment is never His final word. When God cuts sin back, it is always to create room for His grace. How did God show His grace after the Tower of Babel?

_____

_____

Spotlight on Christ

9. How is Jesus Christ reversing the effects of the Tower of Babel? How have you experienced this?

_____

_____

_____

_____

APPLYING

10. _For personal reflection:_ Is there a sin that has taken root in your life? What steps can you take to get it under control?

_____

_____

_____

_____

5
Blood

Read EXODUS 3:1–15; 12:1–13

LAUNCHING

1. From what sources have you derived your mental image of God? How has that image changed over the course of your life?

_____

_____

_____

_____

EXPLORING
God Breaks His Silence

2. Describe briefly what happened during the period between Abraham and Moses. (Use the time line on page 66 as a reminder.)

_____

_____

_____

_____

Why is there

such a strong

emphasis on

blood in the

Bible story?

The Self-Sustaining Fire

3. How did Moses get an accurate picture of God? How can we gain an accurate picture today?

_____

_____

_____

_____

Confusion About God

4. How might Moses' upbringing have created some confusion about who God was?

_____

_____

_____

5. How are these same forces impacting young people in our culture today? How can we combat them?

_____

_____

_____

_____

_____

6. How do people fashion a god to their liking today? Are there aspects of God's character that you find difficult to accept? How do you handle that?

_____

_____

_____

_____

_____

The Living God and the Other gods

7. What do the plagues reveal about God and His character?

A Blood Sacrifice in Egypt

8. What danger was looming for all those in Egypt as the Passover approached? What danger looms for everyone today? What would it take for people to realize the danger?

Spotlight on Christ

9. How is the Passover a foreshadowing of Jesus as the "Lamb of God"?

APPLYING

10. Imagine God's judgment coming through your community like it did through Egypt. Would it pass over you or descend upon you? Why?

Praise Jesus Christ today as the Lamb of God who will bring you safely through the judgment of God.

6

Law

Read EXODUS 20:1–21

LAUNCHING

1. What were some of the rules of the house when you were growing up? Why do you suppose your parents chose to emphasize those rules?

_____

_____

_____

_____

_____

EXPLORING

A New Dimension of God's Grace

2. What would you say to someone who was trying to obey the Ten Commandments in an effort to get to heaven? If we are not saved by keeping the Law, why is it important?

_____

_____

_____

_____

What is

the role of

the Law in

the life of

a Christian?

Get a Glimpse of the Glory of God!

3. Give a specific example of how our obedience to one of the Ten Commandments reflects the glory of God to the world.

   _____

   _____

   _____

The Greatest Battles of Your Heart

4. Which of the Ten Commandments do you think are most difficult for people to
   obey? Why?

   _____

   _____

   _____

   _____

Learning from the Teacher

5. How can the difficulty in obeying the Ten Commandments drive a person to
   Christ? What implications does this have for presenting the gospel?

   _____

   _____

   _____

   _____

   _____

Laying Track for the Train

6. The Holy Spirit makes it possible to live the Christian life. In practical terms,
   how can we draw upon the power of the Holy Spirit to obey God's commands?

   _____

   _____

   _____

Spotlight on Christ

7. How does faith in Jesus Christ turn the commands of God into promises of God? How have you experienced this in your own life?

_____

_____

_____

_____

_____

8. We encountered three pictures of the Law in this chapter. Briefly, describe how the Law is like a mirror, an X ray, and a train track.

_____

_____

_____

_____

_____

APPLYING

9. How has this lesson changed your perspective on the Ten Commandments?

_____

_____

_____

_____

10. Find a place to be alone with God. Read through the Ten Commandments and pray that God would use them to show you anything in your life you need to change. Then pray the prayer found on page 87 in response.

Optional Small Group Exercise:
Read the Ten Commandments aloud as a group. Pause after each one, and praise God for His attribute it reflects.

7
Atonement

Read EXODUS 32

LAUNCHING

1. Do you think people experience guilt today? How do they deal with it?

_____

_____

_____

EXPLORING
Felt Needs and Market Forces

2. How did catering to "felt needs" and "market forces" lead Aaron to make tragic leadership decisions? What would a church emphasize today if it catered to "felt needs" and "market forces"? Do you see this happening today in the church? How?

_____

_____

_____

_____

_____

What is

atonement

and why

is it necessary?

The Mindless Party

3. Why did the Israelites so quickly fall away from God? How could people be susceptible to the same temptation today?

_____

_____

_____

_____

The Meaning of Atonement

4. Why didn't God simply forgive the people when they were sorry?

_____

_____

_____

5. Define atonement in your own words.

_____

_____

_____

A Great Leader Can't Do It

6. Three strategies proved to be unsuccessful in restoring God's presence (pages 95–97): being sorry, the intercession of another human being, and painstaking obedience. Describe how you see people using these same attempts to restore their relationship with God today.

_____

_____

_____

_____

_____

A Worthy Sacrifice Will Do It

7. What finally did restore God's presence? Why was this successful when all of the other attempts failed?

Spotlight on Christ

8. What did Jesus have to do to restore our relationship with God?

APPLYING

9. Check the strategies you most often employ to try and restore your relationship with God after you have sinned.

O Beating myself up over my failure

O Keeping some distance from God until His displeasure passes

O Committing myself to trying harder so that God will forgive me

O Commiserating with someone to get reassurance that I am O.K.

O Looking to a pastor, priest or other religious figure for forgiveness

O Other: _____

10. According to what you learned in this chapter, how should you respond when you sin?

Optional Small Group Exercise:

Take a few minutes to privately write down any sins you have committed that still cause you lingering guilt. Next write out 1 Peter 3:18 on the paper and fold it up. Collect all of the papers and destroy them. Let this mark in your mind that your sin is atoned for and forgiven only through the atonement of Jesus Christ.

8
Priest

Read LEVITICUS 16

LAUNCHING

1. Can you think of a time that someone forgave you when you did not deserve it? How did that make you feel?

_____

_____

_____

_____

EXPLORING

Meeting with God

2. How was the mercy of God and the justice of God portrayed in the Day of Atonement?

_____

_____

_____

_____

What does

God do

with our sins

when we

confess them?

3. List the emotions and thoughts that would have run through your mind as you watched each act of the drama of the Day of Atonement unfold . . .

a. as the priest appeared dressed like a slave

b. when the priest sacrificed a bull for his own sin

c. when atonement was made

d. when the priest prayed the prayer of confession

e. when you watched the guilty goat disappear over the horizon

4. Which of these "acts" would have seemed particularly moving to you?

5. The central truths vividly portrayed in the Day of Atonement are summarized on the bottom of page 108. Discuss how each of these truths point forward to Jesus Christ.

Spotlight on Christ
6. What new insights did you gain about Jesus Christ and His work on the cross from examining the events of the Day of Atonement?

7. Jesus Christ's death on the cross is sufficient to cover the sins of the whole world. But we must apply it to our sins in particular. How would you explain to someone how to do this? (Page 112 provides a sample prayer that might help.)

_____

_____

_____

_____

APPLYING

8. In this chapter we encountered Sarah, who is struggling with a guilty conscience. Do you think there are many Christians like Sarah today? What advice would you give them?

_____

_____

_____

_____

9. Are there any sins that you have trouble believing are forgiven? If so, which ones?

_____

_____

_____

10. Why is it difficult to believe God has forgiven these sins?

_____

_____

_____

Find a time you can spend a few unhurried minutes alone with the Lord. Picture your sin being transferred to the cross. Now read 1 John 1:9 and Psalm 103:11–12. Rest on these promises.

9
Blessing

Read LEVITICUS 26

LAUNCHING

1. Describe how someone in your life has loved you unconditionally.

_____

_____

_____

_____

EXPLORING

God's Unconditional Love

2. Why does God love us, according to Deuteronomy 7:7–8? What new insight does this give you into the unconditional nature of God's love?

_____

_____

_____

_____

_____

_____

If God's love is unconditional, why does obedience matter?

Why Obedience Matters

3. If God loves us unconditionally, what difference does it make if we obey Him or not? How have you seen evidence of this principle operating in your own life?

The Love That Won't Let Go

4. How is God's discipline (bringing calamity upon us when we disobey) actually another expression of His unconditional love for us? Do you think you have ever experienced this in your life?

Agreeing with God's Curses

5. Renouncing sin at Mount Ebal was an essential step to entering into God's blessing. Why might some have been reluctant to endorse God's curses on sin and disobedience? What advice would you give them?

---

6. What did God promise to those who were obedient to His commands? Do you think this principle is still in operation today?

---

7. What does God's blessing look like in our world today?

Spotlight on Christ

8. Jesus said, "I have come that they may have life, and have it to the full." (John 10:10). In what ways have you found that obedience to Christ leads to blessing in your life?

APPLYING

9. Rate yourself from 1 to 10 in relation to your obedience to God over the last ten years, with 1 meaning very disobedient and 10 meaning very obedient. Explain your answer.

10. What changes would you need to make to rate higher over the next ten years?

10
Courage

Read NUMBERS 13:17–14:25

LAUNCHING

1. When you look back at the end of your life, what are one or two things you would like to be able to say?

_____

_____

_____

_____

EXPLORING

Grumbling and Complaining

2. The Israelites under Moses missed their calling and became a group of wandering, aimless people who marked time for a generation. Do you think Christians of your generation face the same danger? Why or why not?

_____

_____

_____

_____

_____

How can we contribute to advancing God's purpose in the world?

3. How did complaining and complacent leadership contribute to the Israelites' failure to fulfill God's calling?

_____

_____

_____

4. If the people of God are to advance God's purpose, they must be thankful, and their leaders must be people of faith. Evaluate a ministry or church you are involved with according to these two criteria. How can you contribute to building a spirit of thanksgiving and faith?

_____

_____

_____

_____

Casting Your Vote for Costly Obedience
5. How was the Israelites' failure to move into the Promised Land a demonstration of contempt toward God? How are we in danger of this today?

_____

_____

_____

Understanding Your Calling
6. In order to avoid an aimless life, we need to be certain of our calling. If someone followed you around for one month, what would that person likely conclude your goal in life was?

○ Being comfortable   ○ Being happy   ○ Being popular

○ Being successful   ○ Having a good family   ○ Being safe and secure

○ Obeying Christ   ○ Other _____

What do you want your goal to be? _____

_____

Counting the Cost

7. There is always a cost associated with obedience. Which of the bulleted statements on page 134 is most difficult for you to affirm? Why?

_____

_____

Spotlight on Christ

8. How did Jesus demonstrate an unwavering commitment to His calling and
a willingness to pay any cost? Why was He willing to do this? What was the
ultimate outcome?

_____

_____

_____

APPLYING

9. Write a mission statement for your life. This should describe in three or four
sentences what you believe God has called you to do. Try and use Scriptures
when possible. Be ready to share it with your small group.

_____

_____

_____

_____

_____

10. Evaluate the activities you are involved with to see if they are helping to advance
the mission God has given you. What do you need to eliminate from or add to
your schedule?

_____

_____

_Read through the prayer on page 136. If it truly expresses the desire of your heart, pray it
to the Lord._

11
Giving
Read DEUTERONOMY 15

LAUNCHING

1. How do you think it would impact your life if you un-
   expectedly inherited $5 million?

_____

_____

_____

_____

How can you

stay spiritually

healthy in

a materialistic

culture?

EXPLORING

Practice Giving

2. What does it mean to be a cheerful giver? How can our
   giving be an act of worship?

_____

_____

_____

_____

_____

3. According to Jesus in Matthew 6:21, what is the relationship between our giving and our hearts? How have you seen this principle operate in your own life?

_____

_____

_____

_____

Restrain Greed

4. How could the Sabbath day and Sabbath year on the land restrain greed? Why would it take faith to follow these stipulations?

_____

_____

_____

_____

5. How could a Sabbath day of rest set margins for your life and activity? What would that look like?

_____

_____

_____

_____

Canceling Debts

6. How would the laws about canceling debts, releasing slaves, and the Year of Jubilee promote compassion and kindness in society? Could these principles be applied today?

_____

_____

_____

_____

Ignoring the Law

7. Why do you think the Year of Jubilee was never practiced? What objections would you anticipate to a law like the Year of Jubilee being proposed today?

Spotlight on Christ

8. How did Jesus fulfill the intentions of the Year of Jubilee to release the oppressed, forgive debts, and bring God's favor?

APPLYING

9. If Jesus reviewed your checkbook ledger and your credit card statements over the last year, what would He conclude about your heart?

10. Set a goal for what you think the Lord would like you to give this year. What changes would you need to make in order to reach that goal? What impact do you think this would have on your heart?

This week, when you give money to your church or another charitable organization, strive to make it an act of worship and devotion to Christ.

12
Evil

Read DEUTERONOMY 19

LAUNCHING

1. In what ways do you see evil at work in our world today?

_____

_____

_____

_____

How can we create a culture that is conducive to holiness?

EXPLORING

A Culture That Encourages Righteous Living

2. How can the church promote a culture that encourages righteous living?

_____

_____

_____

_____

_____

Protecting the Vulnerable/Restraining the Wicked

3. How did the Old Testament law protect the vulnerable (page 153) and restrain the wicked (page 155)?

_____

_____

_____

4. The most extreme punishment, the death penalty, was used to protect three central pillars of society: the worship of God, the sanctity of life, and the sanctity of marriage. How can these pillars best be protected in our society today?

_____

_____

_____

_____

Don't Blame the Government

5. The government has the power and responsibility to create a culture of peace and safety, but it will never be able to create a culture conducive to holiness. Why is that?

_____

_____

_____

_____

The Culture of a Godly Family and an Authentic Church

6. In the chart below, indicate ways the family and church can protect the vulnerable, restrain wickedness, and restore the penitent.

	THE FAMILY	THE CHURCH
Protect the Vulnerable		
Restrain Wickedness		
Restore the Penitent		

Spotlight on Christ

7. In what way has Christ broken the power of evil?

_____

_____

_____

_____

8. In what way does the power of evil remain in our world today?

_____

_____

_____

_____

APPLYING

9. What adjustments can you make in your family life to create a culture more conducive to holiness?

_____

_____

_____

_____

10. What kinds of relationships would help you in your pursuit of holiness? How can you begin to develop this network of relationships?

_____

_____

_____

_____

Optional Small Group Exercise:

As a small group, discuss in very practical terms how you can more effectively create a culture that promotes holiness. Make a plan for implementing this.

13
Covenant

Read JOSHUA 24

LAUNCHING

1. Describe when and how you came to know Jesus Christ as your Savior and Lord.

_____

_____

_____

_____

How can we

keep our

covenants

with God?

EXPLORING
Renewing Your Spiritual Commitment

2. What exactly does it mean to serve the Lord? How would you rate your service to the Lord now on a scale from one to ten? Explain your answer.

_____

_____

_____

_____

_____

Remembering God's Faithfulness

3. Joshua gave the people four strategies that would help them to reignite their spiritual passion and keep their covenant with God. The first was to remember God's faithfulness. Use the time line at the beginning of the chapter to recount how God had been faithful to the people of Israel so far.

_____

_____

_____

_____

4. Draw a time line of your life showing the circumstances in which you have especially been aware of God's faithfulness to you.

_____

_____

_____

_____

Make a Decisive Commitment

5. Which of the "gods of this age" particularly vie for the top priority in your life?

_____

_____

_____

_____

6. What would you want your epitaph to say? What could stop you from receiving that epitaph?

_____

_____

_____

_____

Throw Out Your Idols

7. What are you holding on to that keeps you from fully serving the Lord? What would it mean for you to throw out these idols?

_____

_____

_____

_____

Hold Each Other Accountable

8. How can the accountability of other Christians help keep you from forsaking your covenant to the Lord? How have you experienced this in your Christian life up to this point?

_____

_____

_____

_____

Spotlight on Christ

9. What has God promised in His covenant with us through Jesus? What are our obligations in this covenant?

_____

_____

_____

_____

APPLYING

10. If you are sensing that your spiritual life is slipping, take some time this week to be alone with the Lord and walk through the four steps described on page 171. Share with your small group how doing this has impacted your commitment to Christ.

_____

_____

14
Deliverer

Read JUDGES 2

LAUNCHING

1. If you asked your neighbors, coworkers, or fellow students to describe God, what responses would you expect to hear?

_____

_____

_____

_____

_____

What is idolatry,

and how is it

practiced in

America today?

EXPLORING
A Generation Who Did Not Know the Lord

2. What factors might have contributed to a whole generation of "God's people" growing up without knowing the Lord?

_____

_____

_____

_____

_____

3. How do you see these same factors operating today? What can be done to reverse this trend?

_____

_____

_____

Priorities for Parents

4. We are to teach our children who God is and what He has done. Below, list five things from each of these categories that you think would be especially important to teach.

Who God Is: *What God Has Done:*

1. _____   1. _____

2. _____   2. _____

3. _____   3. _____

4. _____   4. _____

5. _____   5. _____

5. What are some creative methods or activities you have found helpful to communicate with children about who God is and what He has done?

_____

_____

_____

Identifying the Idols/The Attraction of Idols

6. How is the phenomenon described in the *Wall Street Journal* article an example of idolatry in America? What do you think compels people to come up with their own quirky conceptions of God?

_____

_____

_____

7. Are there dimensions of God's character that you tend to ignore or downplay? Why?

_____

_____

_____

_____

The God Who Delivers

8. God creates a crisis in order to bring His people back to Himself. Can you see ways in which this has happened in the last one hundred years?

_____

_____

_____

_____

Spotlight on Christ

9. How was Jesus similar to and different from the deliverers of the Old Testament?

_____

_____

_____

_____

APPLYING

10. What can you do to more effectively pass on the knowledge of God to the next generation? Take one of the attributes you recorded from question 4 (Under "Who God Is"), and make a plan to creatively communicate this truth about God to a child in your life.

_____

_____

_____

_____

15
Redeemer

Read RUTH
(It will only take about fifteen minutes!)

LAUNCHING

1. Describe a time when the events of your life made you question what God was doing. Now, looking back, does it make more sense?

_____

_____

_____

_____

_____

_____

EXPLORING
Call Me "Miss Bitter"

2. List the hardships and difficulties that Naomi experienced. How did they impact her?

_____

_____

_____

_____

Why do

we need a

Redeemer?

3. How have the pain and difficulties you have observed and experienced through life impacted you and your relationship with God?

_____

_____

_____

_____

Love That Chooses to Pay a Price

4. What do you admire about Ruth? Is there something from her character you would like to emulate in your own life?

_____

_____

_____

_____

5. Both Ruth and Naomi experienced severe pain and disappointment. Naomi became bitter, but Ruth loved God and others. What makes the difference? How can you be like Ruth rather than Naomi?

_____

_____

_____

_____

_____

The Infectious Power of Kindness

6. What can we learn from Boaz and his kindness to Ruth, a foreigner?

_____

_____

_____

_____

7. Describe a time you experienced a kinship with someone of a different race or nationality because of your common bond in Jesus Christ or a time you experienced a feeling of being "part of the family" at church because of kindness shown by someone there.

8. Think of a nation or race that you would consider an adversary to your own. How would people respond if someone from this nationality walked into your church this Sunday?

Spotlight on Christ

9. What was required for Boaz to be Ruth's kinsman-redeemer? How is this a picture of Jesus Christ our Redeemer?

Applying

10. Are there circumstances in your life that are difficult or do not seem to make sense? How can you apply what you have learned to those situations?

Optional Small Group Exercise:

Pray that God will give each of you an opportunity to reach out to someone in need with an anonymous act of kindness. Share what happened next time in your group.

16

King

Read 1 SAMUEL 8

LAUNCHING

1. Make a time line of your life with the key choices that have brought you to where you are today. Share this with the group.

_____

_____

_____

_____

_____

Why did God not want His people to have a king?

EXPLORING

2. Using the time line on page 198, review the major events of the Bible story from the Exodus through Israel's most famous kings: Saul, David, and Solomon.

_____

_____

_____

_____

The Frustrations of Living by Faith
3. Why do you think the people wanted a king? What was wrong with their request?

_____

_____

_____

_____

The Significance of Choices
4. Why didn't God simply overrule their bad judgment?

_____

_____

_____

_____

5. How does the story of the kings remind us that a bad choice cannot put an end either to God's grace or His purpose for our lives? How have you seen this principle in your own life or in the lives of others?

_____

_____

_____

_____

_____

6. How can we avoid making bad choices and make godly ones instead?

_____

_____

_____

_____

Leadership Qualifications

7. In the left-hand column, fill in the leadership qualities for kings and Christian leaders. Then use these qualifications to evaluate King David, a leader you respect, and yourself.

LEADERSHIP QUALIFICATIONS	KING DAVID	A LEADER YOU RESPECT	YOURSELF	JESUS CHRIST
Anointed by God				

8. In which of these categories do you think Christian leaders most commonly fail today? Which of these are areas of vulnerability in your life?

_____

_____

Spotlight on Christ

9. Jesus came to be the true king of the Jews. Record on the above chart how Jesus uniquely fulfills the royal profile.

APPLYING

10. Which of these areas of leadership do you need to shore up in order to be a more godly leader? How can you do that?

_____

_____

Optional Exercise:

While alone with the Lord, record on paper any regrettable decisions from the past that you fear have compromised your usefulness to the Lord. Destroy the paper and thank the Lord that He is with you and able to use you in your present circumstances just as He did with the nation of Israel. Commit to serving Him with all your heart in the future.

17

Throne

Read 2 SAMUEL 7

LAUNCHING

1. Think of someone you would describe as genuinely humble. What does humility look like in this person's life?

_____

_____

_____

_____

Where should

we look for

stability and

security?

EXPLORING

God with King David

2. How did King David place God at the center of national life? What would it look like to place God at the center of national life today?

_____

_____

_____

_____

_____

The Test of Humility

3. From what you learned in this chapter, how would you define humility in your own words? How was King David an example of this?

4. Think of a project, ministry, or activity you are involved with. What would it look like for you to express humility in this endeavor?

Disappointment and the Door of Promise

5. David's disappointment in not building the temple was eclipsed by a much greater promise from God. Share a time when you wanted to do something good but God closed the door. How was this disappointment a door to God's blessing?

6. List the three elements of the promise given to David in 2 Samuel 7:13–14. Why would it be impossible for a human king to fulfill these?

Spotlight on Christ

7. Describe how Jesus uniquely fulfills each of the promises given to David.

_____

_____

The Bible's Greatest Miracle

8. What new insights did you gain about the Incarnation—God taking on human flesh in Jesus Christ—in this lesson?

_____

_____

_____

Children of God

9. Which of the bulleted truths on page 220 are especially meaningful to you? Why?

_____

_____

_____

APPLYING

10. Pray this week for someone who is involved in a ministry, activity, or job similar to yours. Pray that God would bless that person greatly for His honor and glory. Describe how this affects your own heart and humility.

_____

_____

_____

In your quiet times with the Lord this week, take one of the bulleted truths from page 220 and turn it into a prayer of praise and thanksgiving.

Optional Small Group Exercise:

Read Revelation 5:9–10, 13 out loud. Use these verses to transition you into a time of praise and worship of Jesus, who sits on the throne of the universe forever.

18
Prophet

Read 2 SAMUEL 12:1–14

LAUNCHING

1. Describe a time when you felt that God was speaking to you.

_____

_____

_____

_____

_____

_____

How has

God spoken

to us?

EXPLORING

The Terrors of Hearing the Voice of God

2. God sent the prophet Nathan to confront David's hidden sin. How was this an expression of His grace?

_____

_____

_____

_____

The Role of a Prophet

3. Read 2 Peter 1:20–21. What do we learn from these verses about the way God gave His Word to the prophets? What do you think this experience was like for the prophets?

4. How has understanding this process impacted your view of the Old Testament?

5. Describe how Nathan fulfilled the role of the prophet with David.

Spotlight on Christ

6. Read Hebrews 1:1–2. How has God "spoken to us by his Son"?

7. How is the role of the prophet in the Old Testament fulfilled by the Holy Spirit today?

8. How does God speak today? What helps you to be receptive?

APPLYING

9. *For personal reflection:* Is God pointing out something in your life that is displeasing to Him?

10. Are you responding more like King David or Herod?

King David asked God to search his heart. Use his words, recorded in Psalm 139:23–24, to shape your own prayer. Record anything the Lord brings to mind.

19
Temple

Read 1 KINGS 8

LAUNCHING

1. At what times and places do you especially sense God's presence?

_____

_____

_____

_____

_____

_____

Where can

we go to meet

with God?

EXPLORING

Seeking God's Presence

2. Using the time line on page 17, trace the history of God's presence and how it was revealed through "theophanies" in the Bible story.

_____

_____

_____

_____

God's Stonecutters

3. The Bible describes Christians as living stones for the eternal temple. What "stonecutters" has God used (or perhaps is still using) in your life to shape you to be more like Christ?

_____

_____

_____

_____

4. How would it change your attitude toward difficult people or painful events in your life if you were able to view them as God's stonecutters?

_____

_____

_____

Responding with Worship

5. What would you have thought and felt if you had seen the cloud of God's presence fill the temple? Why?

_____

_____

_____

_____

The Sad Story of the Temple

6. How was the spiritual life of God's people affected when the Ark of the Covenant was lost?

_____

_____

_____

_____

Spotlight on Christ

7. How is Jesus Christ like the temple today? How does this make our relationship with God today different than that of people in the Old Testament?

8. How are Christian believers like the temple today?

9. The cloud of God's presence filling the temple is a picture of God's Spirit filling you. In what situations do you most need the confidence of knowing that God is with you?

APPLYING

10. Take a moment to identify God's stonecutters in your life. You may want to tell Him how painful they are for you. Ask the Lord to use the trials in your life to shape you for ministry now and prepare you for entering His presence.

Optional Small Group Exercise:

Commit to memorizing 1 Corinthians 6:19 as a group. Agree on a day when each member of the group will intentionally meditate on this truth. Record how the exercise impacted the day.

20
Worship

Read 1 KINGS 18:16–40

LAUNCHING

1. What helps you to worship God authentically?

_____

_____

EXPLORING

Planting the Seeds of Division

2. Solomon started off well but finished horribly. On the chart below, record how Solomon slid into these dangerous pitfalls. Then record how you have seen a contemporary leader fall into one of these errors, and how you might be susceptible to these same mistakes.

	SOLOMON	CONTEMPORARY LEADER	YOURSELF
Losing Touch with Hurting People			
Sliding into Indulgence			
Doing What's Popular			

What are the distinguishing marks of authentic worship?

A Turning of the Tide

3. In half a century, Israel had gone from a nation loyal to the living God to a divided and confused nation where religion was a matter of personal choice. How have you seen this same progression happening in your country? What consequences have resulted from this?

_____

_____

_____

_____

_____

_____

Authentic Worship Is a Response to Revealed Truth

4. How did Elijah's demand for the people to decide which God they would follow fly in the face of the prevailing philosophy of religious tolerance? Would it have been more loving for Elijah to have affirmed the personal faith of the prophets of Baal?

_____

_____

_____

_____

Authentic Worship Focuses on the Living God

5. How would you answer someone who said that it does not matter which God you worship as long as you are sincere? How might the story of Elijah and the prophets of Baal help you in your answer?

_____

_____

_____

_____

_____

6. God revealed His greatness and glory to the people at Mount Carmel by sending fire from heaven. What has helped you to have a greater grasp of God's glory?

_____

_____

_____

Authentic Worship Focuses on an Acceptable Sacrifice

7. The worshipers and prophets of Baal deserved judgment, yet God's fire fell on the sacrifice rather than the people. What attributes of God did this reveal to those assembled?

_____

_____

_____

Spotlight on Christ

8. How can we keep our worship focused on what Christ has done for us on the Cross?

_____

_____

_____

APPLYING

9. Is there something you need to change in your life to keep from following in the footsteps of Solomon?

_____

_____

_____

10. How can you worship God more authentically?

_____

_____

_____

21
Sin

Read 2 KINGS 17

What is sin

and why is

it serious?

LAUNCHING

1. How would you go about trying to convince Bob, the thirty-five-year-old husband and father, that he is, in fact, a sinner?

_____

_____

_____

_____

_____

EXPLORING

The Priority of Godliness and Righteousness

2. Define godliness and righteousness in your own words. What is their relationship?

_____

_____

_____

_____

_____

3. The northern kingdom became a cesspool of sin, violence, and moral confusion. What set them on this track? What could have reversed its course?

4. What would you say to someone who claimed the solution to the problems of our society today lies in more moral instruction and character education?

Bob's Biggest Problem: Life Without God

5. How can someone like Bob, who is a faithful family man, trying to live a good life, ultimately be under God's wrath and judgment? How have the principles from this chapter changed the way you view "good" people like Bob?

Provoking the Anger of God

6. How is God's love different from His anger? What attributes of God are revealed by His anger?

7. What was the result of God's anger toward the northern kingdom? How is this a picture of the predicament faced by people who are rejecting Him today?

_____

_____

_____

_____

Spotlight on Christ

8. What can we learn about communicating the Good News from Jesus' interaction with the woman at the well?

_____

_____

_____

_____

APPLYING

9. What do you need to do to take sin more seriously in your life?

_____

_____

_____

10. How did the truths from this lesson impact the way you see those around you who do not know Christ as their personal Savior? What will you do in response?

_____

_____

_____

_____

Optional Small Group Exercise:
Have someone take the role of Bob, and let the others in the group try to share the gospel with him.

22
Righteousness

Read 2 KINGS 23:1–28

LAUNCHING

1. What has shaped your understanding of right and wrong?

_____

_____

_____

_____

EXPLORING

The Influence of a Godly Leader

2. Josiah grew up without any kind of spiritual heritage. What do you think caused this young man to begin seeking the Lord? How do you see signs of this same thing happening today in the lives of young people?

_____

_____

_____

_____

_____

What is righteousness and how can it be established in our land?

3. Josiah wanted to turn his country back to the living God. He made many changes, but they did not last. Knowing how the story ended, what advice would you have given Josiah?

_____

_____

_____

Rediscovering the Bible
4. The religious leaders of Josiah's day ran the temple without the Word of God. Would it be possible to run a church without using the Bible today? Have you seen this happen? What were the results?

_____

_____

_____

_____

Rediscovering Right and Wrong
5. Is there confusion in your culture about what is right and wrong? If so, why?

_____

_____

What would it take to reverse this trend?

_____

_____

_____

6. What would you say to someone who said, "That may be wrong for you, but it is not wrong for me"?

_____

_____

_____

7. How do you decide whether something is right or wrong? Are there areas where you find it particularly difficult to determine right and wrong? Why?

_____

_____

_____

_____

Leading a Reformation

8. In what sense was Josiah's campaign of reform a success and in what sense was it a failure? Why? What would it take to bring righteousness back to our nation?

_____

_____

_____

_____

Spotlight on Christ

9. How can a person be right with God?

_____

_____

_____

APPLYING

10. Growing in righteousness involves removing what displeases God from our lives and developing a lifestyle that is modeled on the character of Jesus. Try to identify a next step for your own growth in righteousness.

_____

_____

Optional Small Group Exercise:
Point out signs of God's work you can observe in the lives of each of the members of your small group.

23
Joy
Read NEHEMIAH 8

LAUNCHING

1. Describe a time you felt a great sense of joy. What was it about that experience that made you joyful?

_____

_____

_____

_____

_____

_____

How can

God's people

experience

His joy?

EXPLORING

2. Using the time line on page 17 as a guide, review the history of God's people. You should now have a good sense of the key landmarks of the Old Testament story.

_____

_____

_____

_____

Bring Out the Bible!

3. Why did the people have such a strong desire to hear the words of the Bible? What has given you that desire?

_____

_____

_____

_____

The Value of Family Worship

4. What were the benefits of including the children in the worship and teaching session led by Ezra? What are the implications of this for today?

_____

_____

_____

_____

Making the Meaning Clear

5. What made Ezra's teaching so powerfully effective? What does Ezra's example teach us about effective communication and learning in the church today?

_____

_____

_____

_____

6. Why were the people so receptive to Ezra's teaching? What helps you to hear and receive God's Word? What prevents you from hearing?

_____

_____

_____

_____

The Joy of Grace and Obedience

7. God's Word humbled the people, but it also lifted them up and directed them to a new life of obedience. How have you experienced these same effects of the Word of God in your life?

8. How can we experience the joy of the Lord described by Nehemiah? How can this be our strength?

Spotlight on Christ

9. How does Christ bring joy to His people now? How will that joy be different when Christ returns?

APPLYING

10. Where are you looking to find joy in your life? Evaluate your response in light of what you learned from this chapter.

Optional Small Group Exercise:

The people of God joyfully celebrated the Festival of Booths to commemorate God's faithfulness to them. Consider planning an event as a family or small group to celebrate God's goodness and faithfulness.

Since 1894, Moody Publishers has been dedicated to equip and motivate people to advance the cause of Christ by publishing evangelical Christian literature and other media for all ages, around the world. As a ministry of the Moody Bible Institute of Chicago, proceeds from the sale of this book help to train the next generation of Christian leaders.

If we may serve you in any way in your spiritual journey toward understanding Christ and the Christian life, please contact us at www.moodypublishers.com.

"All Scripture is God-breathed and is useful for teaching, rebuking, correcting and training in righteousness, so that the man of God may be thoroughly equipped for every good work."
— 2 Timothy 3:16, 17

MOODY
PUBLISHERS
THE NAME YOU CAN TRUST*

Unlocking the Bible Story Series

Pastor Colin Smith's four-volume masterpiece moves you past Bible stories to understand the Bible as one story—the glorious, unbroken account of Christ's work to redeem a fallen world.

Each chapter of the Unlocking the Bible Story Series, Volumes 1-4 coincide with the same chapters of the Unlocking the Bible Story Study Guides.

Unlocking the Bible Story, Volume 1
Volume 1 takes readers through the Old Testament story from Genesis to Nehemiah.
ISBN: 0-8024-6543-9, Volume 1
ISBN: 0-8024-6551-X, Volume 1, Study Guide

Unlocking the Bible Story, Volume 2
After you have completed Volume 1, Volume 2 is highly recommended as it takes readers through the Old Testament story from Job to Malachi.
ISBN: 0-8024-6544-7, Volume 2
ISBN: 0-8024-6552-8, Volume 2, Study Guide

Unlocking the Bible Story, Volume 3
Volume 3 begins with the coming of the Messiah, Jesus Christ and continues with Christ's ministry and the beginning of the church. Volume 3 will help you unlock the Bible story from Matthew to Acts.
ISBN: 0-8024-6545-5, Volume 3
ISBN: 0-8024-6553-6, Volume 3, Study Guide

Unlocking the Bible Story, Volume 4
Volume 4 takes readers through the letters written to the New Testament churches, which tell the full significance of what God has done in Jesus Christ, and concludes with the revelation of the apostle John, who brings us right into the future city of God.
ISBN: 0-8024-6546-3, Volume 4
ISBN: 0-8024-6554-4, Volume 4, Study Guide

MOODY
PUBLISHERS
THE NAME YOU CAN TRUST.

1-800-678-6928 www.MoodyPublishers.com

UNLOCKING THE BIBLE STORY STUDY GUIDE TEAM

ACQUIRING EDITOR:
William Thrasher

COPY EDITOR:
Jim Vincent

BACK COVER COPY:
The Smartt Guys

COVER DESIGN:
The Smartt Guys

INTERIOR DESIGN:
Paetzold Associates

PRINTING AND BINDING:
Data Reproductions Corporation

The typeface for the text of this book is
Goudy